CO

CW00838801

INTRODUCTION.......

THE ROUTES

SOME USEFUL ADDRESSES

Yorkshire Dales National Park Authority
Colvend, Hebden Road, Grassington, Skipton BD23 5LB
(01756-752748)

Information Centres
Car Park, Hebden Road **Grassington** (01756-752774)
35 Coach Street **Skipton** (01756-792809)
Station Road **Ilkley** (01943-602319)

Yorkshire Dales Society
Otley Civic Centre, Cross Green, Otley LS21 1HD
(01943-461938)

Cyclists' Touring Club
Cotterell House, 69 Meadrow, Godalming, Surrey GU7 3HS
(01483-417217)

British Cycling Federation
National Cycling Centre, Stuart Street, Manchester M11 4DQ
(0161-2302301)

Sustrans
Crown House, 37-41 Prince Street, Bristol BS1 4PS
(0117-927 7555)

INTRODUCTION

Wharfedale is the most popular valley in the Yorkshire Dales, helped by being highly accessible from most West Yorkshire and East Lancashire conurbations. The landscape of Wharfedale is a rich and varied one, offering sometimes startling contrasts between sombre gritstone and gleaming limestone: both forms are experienced during these rides. At the very heart of the dale is the small town of Grassington, from where roads, tracks and paths radiate in every possible direction. All the rides begin within a few short miles of this characterful location.

Given that Wharfedale is one of the major valleys of the Yorkshire Dales, it is interesting to note that the majority of biking opportunities fall within only one part of it. North of Kilnsey the valley floor is dead flat and narrow between steep flanks, leaving little in the way of sensible gradients. Similarly, the entrance to the dale around Bolton Abbey is guarded by the huge portals of Barden Moor and Barden Fell. So it is that the most practicable biking routes fall largely in mid-Wharfedale. The Grassington area boasts a splendid network of routes of which many have been traced, researched and drawn into this guide. Each of the rides links bridleways and country lanes, with a minimum of time spent on busier roads. All the selected rides are based on *sensible* routes: the presence of a bridleway on the map doesn't always guarantee that it's worth using.

There is no escaping the fact that this is hilly country: all of these routes feature uphill sections, though some are gentler than others, and the more arduous sections are mostly short-lived. While ground conditions vary with the season and the weather, most people will enjoy the majority of their outings in the warmer months. Don't be surprised to find a dry July run transformed into a muddy December struggle. None of these rides, however, should involve too much slutchy work, though in some cases there may be a short spell where the only option, other than for a superhero, is to get off and push. These have been kept to an absolute minimum: if we'd come to walk, we'd have put our boots on!

The rides are in the 8-13 miles (13-21km) range, with the emphasis firmly on leisure riding rather than endurance test. Mention is sometimes made of shorter or easier options. The ratio of off-road to on-road riding is given for each run, but even the road work is almost exclusively on peaceful country lanes. Even taken at a steady pace, and savouring villages and sights en route, these runs fall into the category of a morning, afternoon or summer's evening ride: for

WHARFEDALE BIKING GUIDE

Pocket Rides

③

Paul Hannon

HILLSIDE

HILLSIDE
PUBLICATIONS
12 Broadlands
Shann Park
Keighley
West Yorkshire
BD20 6HX

First published 2002

© Paul Hannon 2002

ISBN 1 870141 72 5

Illustrations
Front Cover: On Barden Moor
Back Cover: On Moor Lane, Linton
Page 1: Linton
(Paul Hannon/Hillslides Picture Library)

Printed in Great Britain by
Carnmor Print
95-97 London Road
Preston
Lancashire
PR1 4BA

families with younger members, however, I can confirm that the best part of a day might need to be allocated! Most pass a pub or two somewhere along the way, with other refreshment halts sometimes available. Another useful feature is the indication of places of interest along the routes: not all guidebooks believe cyclists have any interest in their surroundings.

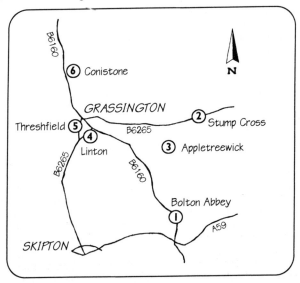

Sadly an irresponsible minority have given bikers a bad name in outdoor circles, which is unfortunate for the responsible majority. As a dedicated hillwalker, I too have had harsh words for mountain bikers carving up public footpaths in beautiful places, and have indeed witnessed such actions in the Yorkshire Dales. To be fair, many people drawn to the countryside for the first time on acquiring a bike are often genuinely unaware of their rights and responsibilities. Hopefully the rides in the following pages will encourage more riders to enjoy a stimulating, entirely legal journey through our countryside, leaving no lasting sign of their passage. The Mountain Bike Code of Conduct is reproduced overleaf, and it incorporates the traditional Country Code. To sum up: ride with care, ride only where you are permitted, and ride with an awareness of the environment and other users of the outdoors within this precious National Park landscape.

THE MOUNTAIN BIKE CODE OF CONDUCT

RIGHTS OF WAY

- *Bridleways* - open to cyclists, but you must give way to walkers and horse riders.

- *Byways* - Usually unsurfaced tracks open to cyclists. As well as walkers and cyclists, you may meet occasional vehicles which also have a right of access.

- *Public footpaths* - no right to cycle exists.

Look out for posts from the highway or waymarking arrows (blue for bridleways, red for byways and yellow for footpaths).

OTHER ACCESS

- *Open land* - on most upland, moorland and farmland cyclists normally have no right of access without the express permission of the landowner

- *Towpaths* - a British Waterways cycling permit is required for cyclists wishing to use their canal towpaths

- *Pavements* - cycling is not permitted on pavements

- *Designated cycle paths* - look out for designated cycle paths or bicycle routes which may be found in urban areas, on Forestry Commission land, disused railway lines or other open spaces

OTHER INFORMATION

- Cyclists must adhere to the Highway Code. A detailed map is recommended for more adventurous trips.

THE COUNTRY CODE

- Enjoy the countryside and respect its life and work
- Guard against all risk of fire
- Fasten all gates
- Keep dogs under close control
- Keep to rights of way across farmland
- Use gates and stiles to cross fences, hedges and walls
- Leave livestock, crops and machinery alone
- Take your litter home
- Help to keep all water clean
- Protect wildlife, plants and trees
- Take special care of country roads
- Make no unnecessary noise

SAFETY

- Ensure that your bike is safe to ride and prepared for all emergencies
- You are required by law to display working lights after dark (front and rear)
- Always carry some form of identification
- Always tell someone where you are going
- Learn to apply the basic principles of first aid
- Reflective materials on your clothes or bike can save your life
- For safety on mountains refer to *Safety on Mountains,* a British Mountaineering Council publication
- Ride under control when going downhill, since this is often when serious accidents occur
- If you intend to ride fast off road it is advisable to wear a helmet
- Particular care should be taken on unstable or wet surfaces

START Bolton Abbey   grid ref. SE 071539
Start from main car park just off the B6160 in the village.

DISTANCE 8¾ miles/14km
Off road 6¼ miles/10km   **On road** 2½ miles/4km

TERRAIN A gently graded ascent by country lane and green lane, rewarded with a superb run of optional duration on a splendid heather moorland track.
The return is entirely off-road and hassle-free.

ORDNANCE SURVEY MAPS
1:50,000 - Landranger 104, Leeds, Bradford & Harrogate
1:25,000 - Explorer OL2, Yorkshire Dales South/West

REFRESHMENTS
Pub and cafe near start.

S Join the minor road behind the shop/Post office, and immediately leave the crowds behind by turning left. This virtually traffic-free little lane winds gently uphill to Halton East. Don't be misled by its condition at Hesketh House: it does pass through the farmyard before resuming through open fields. There may be one or two gates to open and close. To the right are the return slopes of Hare Head, and beyond them Halton Height. At a junction you can detour left to run through the centre of **Halton East**, or simply keep straight on to the minor junction alongside Halton Church Mission Room.

Here turn right down an unsigned road which quickly expires. Keep straight on through the gate in front and onto the track of Moor Lane. This starts to rise between widely spaced walls, becoming grassier as a gentle pull leads to a gate onto the foot of Halton Moor. Pause to enjoy views back to an array of local heights including Skipton Moor, Rombalds Moor and Beamsley Beacon. The main track turns right to contour around then ascend through a trough to arrive at the Embsay-Barden road just beneath the road's summit on Halton Height. Immediately to the north are massive views of Barden Moor over its lower reservoir, with Simon's Seat prominent across Wharfedale.

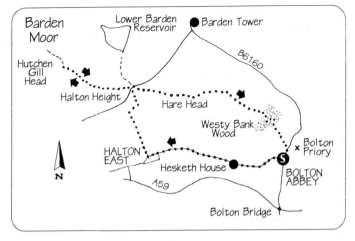

The full route now takes a detour onto **Barden Moor**, making use of a superb bridleway for as long as desired. The bridleway strictly starts from the very brow of the road up to the left, where a broad path rises away, soon swinging down and slanting along to join a firm shooters' track. In practice, most users simply cross straight over the road to commence immediately along the better surfaced shooters' track. This can be followed as far as you like - always remembering you've got to come back. The excellent surface and impressive surroundings certainly encourage progress. Perhaps a good option is to ride for a mile as far as Hutchen Gill Head (the second stream crossing).

Thatched shooters' cabin
at Hutchen Gill Head,
looking over Lower Barden Reservoir to Simon's Seat

Back at the road, descend over the cattle-grid and leave immediately by a gate on the right. A superb grassy track heads off through the heather of Hare Hill Side, and from the next gate runs over rougher pasture to the crest of Middle Hare Head. From here the effort is further repaid with a lengthy downhill return all the way to Bolton Abbey. A word of caution, the first section on departing is moderately steep. Down the rough pasture, a wall leads down to a gate. Head directly away to some water tanks, crossing over a firmer track and slanting down to a gate ahead. Continue down again, faintly through a large field to a gate into Westy Bank Wood. In springtime this is decorated with bluebells.

The Old Hall, Halton East

A firm, broad way zigzags down to quickly leave the trees. Across a small field take the left-hand of two gates, and head away on a faint track to the left of some duckponds. Drop down to the bottom where a gate admits onto a firm access track. Go left on this, to be immediately faced by the very dramatic prospect of Bolton Hall's castellations, and with the priory church itself behind. The road is joined with caution and followed along to the right for two minutes back into **Bolton Abbey** village, concluding under the historic three-arch aqueduct en route.

ALONG THE WAY

• **Halton East** is an attractive, tiny village off the beaten track. Most notable house is the 17th century Old Hall set a short way back from the small green by the junction: its matching south and east fronts feature intricate mullioned and transomed windows. Both central junctions have interesting guideposts: one is topped by an old 'West Riding' sign complete with a grid reference, while by the mission room is a much older stone milestone inscribed to Skipton and Bolton.

Hole in the Wall, Bolton Abbey

• **Barden Moor** is a special tract of upland, a vast playground both for the rambler and the less unobtrusive 'sportsman'. Above the intake walls encircling the moor, bracken flanks give way to heather and rough grass, where one can follow paths and tracks or simply roam free. However, the only place where bikes are welcome is along the Bolton Abbey to Rylstone bridleway, so please don't be tempted to explore any other tracks. The millstone grit outcrops and edges that characterise the northern and western scarps of the moor are absent from the area we see. Both the substantial reservoirs harness Barden Beck which flows from the heart of the moor, and were built to supply the growing thirsts of Bradford.

Tithe Barn, Bolton Abbey

• **Bolton Abbey** is, strictly, the name for the tiny village whose showpiece is more correctly the Priory. The imposing ruin forms a magnet for close-at-hand West Yorkshire visitors, with the River Wharfe hereabouts being an attraction in its own right. The priory dates from 1154 and was built by Augustinian canons who moved here from nearby Embsay. At the Dissolution the nave was spared, and remains to this day the parish church. There is much else of interest in the vicinity, including adjacent Bolton Hall dating from the 17th century, and a large and splendid example of a tithe barn. Visiting the priory from the car park, the first sighting is the classic framed view through the roadside 'Hole in the Wall'.

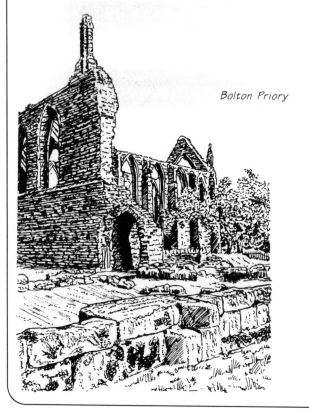

Bolton Priory

START Stump Cross   grid ref. SE 086635
Start from a large lay-by below the steep bend just beneath
Stump Cross Caverns on the Grassington-Pateley Bridge road.

DISTANCE 12¾ miles/20km
Off road 5¾ miles/9km   **On road** 7 miles/11km

TERRAIN A high altitude ride that drops only briefly below the
1000ft contour. The first half is on roads, the return half entirely
off, using an old road across the moors. Note that this is marred
by a short length of unavoidable bogs where you are likely to
get muddy. Very little in the way of appreciable gradients.

ORDNANCE SURVEY MAPS
1:50,000 - Landranger 99, Northallerton & Ripon
Landranger 104, Leeds, Bradford & Harrogate
1:25,000 - Explorer 298, Nidderdale

REFRESHMENTS
Cafe at Stump Cross Caverns, pub at Greenhow.

S From the lay-by set off up the road to **Stump Cross Caverns**, the
first section at the bend being perhaps the steepest of the day. At the
caves the gradient eases for a steady pull over Craven Moor to the
watershed. The National Park is not actually vacated until well past
where the sign is located, while mining remains are prominent on
both sides of the road. The road quickly descends into **Greenhow**,
passing numerous isolated houses. Just past the church turn sharp right
on the Blubberhouses road.

Leaving Greenhow behind, this quickly becomes a straight, fast
high-level road that is largely used by quarry waggons needing gentler
gradients than the B6265 Grassington-Pateley road can offer. Expan-
sive moorland vistas can be enjoyed from the rare comfort of more
than three miles of very gradual descent. On eventual arrival at a
junction at the end of the plantation, turn right on the side road for
West End (Hoodstorth Lane). There are glimpses of Thruscross Reservoir cloaked in plantations over to the left. The back road descends
quite steeply into the head of the **Washburn Valley**. The youthful river

is crossed on a simple bridge at a parking area before winding back up and along to a sharp bend at Red Gate. Here ends the road section.

Take the rough road through the gate on the right, a short pull that ignores a lesser fork left to quickly reach a gate onto the open moor. A useful board imparts information about the surrounds of the Barden Fell Access Area: this particular tract of the moor is evocatively titled The Great Stray. Resume along the track, known as Forest Road, which ultimately links with similar roads leading to Skyreholme and, in our case, Stump Cross. The firm track takes in a dip then rises to enjoy a good level section before a steeper drop to Harden Gill. This attractive corner also features stepping-stones on the stream. The short, steep pull out to a gate is followed by a sustained gentler rise onto **Pock Stones Moor**, reaching the high point with the Little Pock Stones just over to the right.

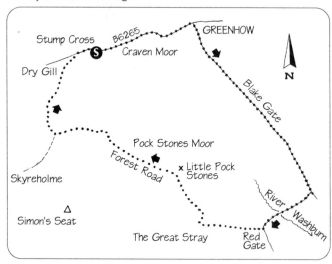

What follows should be a leisurely downhill mile back into the National Park, but sadly its first stage is currently something of a quagmire: the map identifies the several guilty runnels coming off the moor, their presence exacerbated by motorised use of this old road. The awkward spell is actually quite short, though it may not seem that way at the time. A much-improved green way resumes down the slope to reach a gate and the National Park boundary at Eller Edge Nook. Now enclosed by walls, the old road winds down and along to a junction of such ways. Simon's Seat, just across to the left, powerfully dominates the scene hereabouts, with the Skyreholme area in the valley below and Barden Moor across Wharfedale. Arrest the decline by turning right on the good surface of Black Hill Road, again between limestone walls. After a very brief pull (note the limekiln on the right) it runs along to its high point at a gate, before a splendid descent across the moor towards Dry Gill (passing above a cave). The track runs along to meet the Pateley Bridge road just down from the starting point.

ALONG THE WAY

• **Stump Cross Caverns** is one of only three showcaves in the Dales, having been discovered in 1860 by unsuspecting leadminers. They revealed an amazing labyrinth of tunnels and chambers, with a display of stalactites and stalagmites that cannot fail to impress. The bleak exterior and setting give no clues to the wonders underground.

• **Greenhow** is a desolate spot straddling the road summit, and its allegiance lies with Nidderdale - a good sweep of which is visible from here. Variously claimed to be the highest village in Yorkshire, with the highest parish church in England, the Miners Arms at 1243ft/ 379m is certainly second only to Tan Hill (England's highest) in the Dales. Greenhow's origins are based on lead mining on the nearby moors: evidence is everywhere, from the name of the pub to the carving on the roadside war memorial. Coldstones Quarry is an immense modern operation at the eastern end of the village.

• **The Washburn Valley** is an unsung little dale between the Wharfe and the Nidd. The River Washburn flows into the Wharfe on the edge of busy Otley, in stark contrast to its winding miles from moorland beginnings. Here a chain of reservoirs harness the river and its gathering grounds in a manner that has largely blended well into the scene. Highest of these lakes is Thruscross Reservoir, only completed as recently as 1966. Sacrificed in the process was the hamlet of West End, which has since returned to daylight in times of drought.

• **Pock Stones Moor** is part of the vast expanse of heather uplands reaching from Bolton Abbey across the head of the Washburn Valley towards Pateley Bridge, and is equally popular with ramblers and grouse shooters. The Great Pock Stones are a cluster of gritstone boulders to the west of the route's high point at 1410ft/430m. The closer Little Pock Stones are, perversely, far more substantial, and a two-minute stroll out to them makes for a good refreshment break. During the climb to the high point of the moor, Thruscross Reservoir and the 'golf balls' of RAF Menwith Hill are very prominent, while arrival at the top brings views into the heart of the Dales, featuring Fountains Fell, Darnbrook Fell, Old Cote Moor and Great Whernside.

START Appletreewick   grid ref. SE 053601
Start from the village centre.
During the season a large field near the village centre provides
car parking. Other than this, parking is somewhat limited.

DISTANCE 9 miles/14½km
Off road 4½ miles/7¼km   **On road** 4½ miles/7¼km

TERRAIN A good selection of firm green roads in the shadow
of Simon's Seat. The only appreciable uphill work is on
good surfaces, while the downhills are well graded.

ORDNANCE SURVEY MAPS
1:50,000 - Landranger 98, Wensleydale & Upper Wharfedale
Landranger 99, Northallerton & Ripon
1:25,000 - Explorer OL2, Yorkshire Dales South/West

REFRESHMENTS
Two pubs at start, refreshments at Parcevall Hall, just off-route.

S   Leave the village by the road east, ignoring a right branch for
Barden and steadily rising to a fork by a former chapel. Fork right
(signed Parcevall Hall) for **Skyreholme**, passing through the hamlet to
reach a bridge over Skyreholme Beck. **Simon's Seat** rises across to the
right. The left fork runs the short distance to Parcevall Hall. Across the
bridge the road begins a long, steady pull up Skyreholme Bank before
finally losing its surface. The lane levels out to run on to a fork. Bear
left here, and continue over the brow on the welcoming green surface
of Black Hill Road. A brief climb leads to the run's high point at 1150ft/
350m, then drops down towards Dry Gill (amid minor lead mining
remains) to join the Pateley Bridge road (B6265).

Turn left on the road past Dry Gill and on to a junction with New
Road near Fancarl House. Keep straight on over the brow and descend
a short way until a rough road goes off left at a small parking area.
Pause first to absorb the sweeping panorama over Wharfedale to the
mass of Barden Moor. A green lane rapidly forms, losing an enclosing
wall to run an idyllic course to join New Road on a bend. Bear right
very briefly then take a gate on the right (not quite as per map), from

where a wide, stony track crosses the broad upland of Appletreewick Pasture. This boasts an extensive panorama including, clockwise, Barden Moor, the Malhamdale hills, Old Cote Moor, Grassington Moor, Great Whernside and Simon's Seat. Further along, a more intimate picture of the river's environs around Burnsall is revealed.

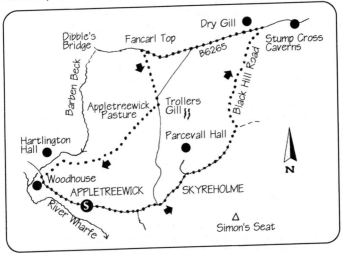

The track drops gently down through gates, and above some barns keep right to drop to a gate onto a short walled section. To the right is the shapely valley of Barben Beck, the outflow from Grimwith Reservoir. The track continues alongside a wall to end at two prominent barns at Kail Gate Lathe. To their right, a mercurial, initially enclosed green way runs on, soon emerging to wind down as Kail Lane.

Note the impressive Hartlington Hall prominent in the trees across the gill, while a little lower we pass a drained circular dewpond, created to slake the thirst of cattle in these otherwise dry limestone surrounds. Just below, the track joins the back road from Appletreewick to Burnsall. Across it is Woodhouse Farm, a 17th century manor house. Re-enter **Appletreewick** by turning left along the road.

ALONG THE WAY

• **Skyreholme** is a scattered farming hamlet with clusters of caravans often in evidence: Lane House Farm on the left is an attractive old place with mullioned windows. Parcevall Hall is the grandest house in Upper Wharfedale. Built over 300 years ago, its beautiful stone-work looks out across Skyreholme to Simon's Seat. Now used as a diocesan retreat centre, the gardens and intermingled woodland are open to the public from Easter to October (fee payable). Reached by footpath only, just a few minutes upstream of the hall is Trollers Gill, a remarkable limestone gorge known as the 'Gordale of Wharfedale'. Though not particularly tall, its cliffs remain unbroken for a consider-able distance. It is renowned as the home of the legendary Barguest, a spectral hound with eyes like saucers!

Trollers Gill, Skyreholme

• **Simon's Seat** totally dominates the Skyreholme area, and our opening couple of miles in particular. Its substantial summit gritstone boss reaches 1591ft/485m, and the fell forms a steep, colourful wall when viewed across the beck. Though a steep path ascends from Skyreholme, it is more commonly climbed from the Cavendish Pavilion at Bolton Abbey, by way of the Valley of Desolation.

• **Appletreewick** has several claims to fame, though many visitors may best remember its delightful name. Here are three halls and two inns in amongst a wonderful assortment of cottages. All stand on or about the narrow road wandering through the village, from High Hall at the top - note the tiny church nearby - to Low Hall at the very bottom. Probably the oldest however is the curiously named Mock Beggar Hall, a fine little edifice that once went by the title of Monk's

Hall. Of the two hostelries, the Craven Arms takes its name from the family of William Craven, a Dick Whittington character who found his fortune in London, becoming Lord Mayor in 1611. Not forgetting his beginnings he became a worthy local benefactor, having Burnsall's grammar school and a number of bridges in the district built. Alongside the pub are the village stocks. The New Inn, meanwhile, achieved national fame in the 1970s thanks to the enterprising 'no-smoking' policy of the then landlord. Today it is equally enterprising in its extensive range of fascinating beers from abroad.

Mock Beggar Hall,
Appletreewick

START Linton   grid ref. SD 997627
Start from the village centre. Parking by the green and
along the road through the village. Can get congested.

DISTANCE 9¾ miles/15½km
Off road 5 miles/8km   **On road** 4¾ miles/7½km

TERRAIN A generally low-level circuit of the old lanes
and villages west of Linton. Very little climbing on
a combination of grassy tracks and firm tracks.

ORDNANCE SURVEY MAPS
1:50,000 - Landranger 98, Wensleydale & Upper Wharfedale
Landranger 103, Blackburn & Burnley
1:25,000 - Explorer OL2, Yorkshire Dales South/West

REFRESHMENTS
Pubs at Linton, Hetton (just off-route); pub and cafe at Cracoe.

S Leave **Linton** village green by crossing the bridge and quickly
forking right on a lesser road (note the old guidepost) rising to join the
B6160 (another old guidepost). Turn right on here for a short spell,
passing the derelict wooden cabins of the former Linton camp school.
Just a little further look out for a gate on the right from where a
bridleway is signed to Thorpe Lane. Ascend this pathless field to the
top left corner, through a gateway and up a field with an impressive
set of lynchets (historic cultivation terraces) to a bridle-gate at the foot
of a narrow enclosed way. This splendid snicket winds up to join the
back road of Thorpe Lane beneath the knoll of Elbolton Hill: in an
uncharacteristic lapse the Ordnance Survey have omitted to portray
this as the enclosed way it has clearly been for a long long time. Note
if wanting to avoid this section remain on the road a little further then
fork right for **Thorpe**, doubling back right again on the edge of the
hamlet, along Thorpe Lane.

Turn right on Thorpe Lane to commence a lengthy spell on this
largely traffic-free byway, much of its first half carrying a grassy central
strip. Sweeping views up the dale feature Old Cote Moor, Buckden
Pike, Great Whernside, Meugher, Grass Wood and Grassington. After

a steep descent several drives are absorbed and the road becomes better surfaced. A sustained rise leads to what is surprisingly the high point of the run, at a modest 869ft/265m. Easy going leads on and down to Threapland, then joining the main road (B6265) on the edge of Cracoe. Note an old inscribed milestone hidden away at the junction.

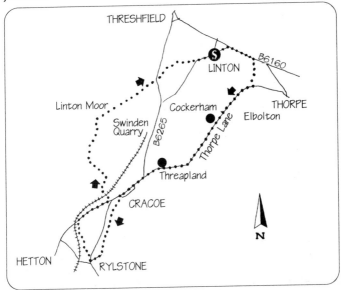

Advance into **Cracoe** and through the village. There is an option to take the first left, then quickly right to trace a back lane through the village, thus avoiding the main road but also its two sources of refreshments. Where this rejoins the main road at a dip at the other end, the Rylstone loop begins. Here turn left up a rough lane rising away, soon levelling out to run a splendid course to Rylstone as Chapel Lane. Part way along note the base of a former wayside cross. By the trees at the end use the gate ahead and advance along the fieldside, noting on the left the grassed over banks still supporting some ancient fishponds. Just past Manor House Farm on the right take a gate onto the drive, and turn right down this narrow road past the church onto the main road again. Straight across is the pond at **Rylstone**.

The route turns right for a few yards on the main road, then branches off at a parking area on the left. From a gate in the corner an inviting green way known rather unfairly as Mucky Lane heads off, a seemingly unfrequented route largely between hedgerows. It emerges at the other end to run along a fieldside between railway line and cricket field to join the Hetton road at a level crossing at the old Rylstone station.

Turn right on here, passing Cracoe's new village hall to reach the main road junction on the edge of Cracoe, marked by an old guidepost. Now turn sharp left down a rough byway, Swinden Lane, and at the bottom keep straight on under the railway line and up the other side. Once the branch line from Skipton to Grassington, the railway survives to serve Swinden Quarry. When the cart track ends at a gate, take a gate on the left to follow a continuing enclosed, seldom-used grassy way rising away. This winds up to emerge into an open field. A fainter way slants up this to a wall corner opposite, then runs on to a gateway at the rear of a prominent barn. This makes a good place for a break, the rear of the nearby massive Swinden Quarry all too evident but nevertheless emphatically overlooked by Cracoe Fell on Barden Moor. Other prominent features include Great Whernside, Grassington, Grassington Moor, Cracoe, Flasby Fell and distant Pendle Hill.

Through the gateway descend the rough pasture to the right side of a pocket of woodland below. Descend through a gateway and with caution down to ford Eller Beck. Turn briefly upstream then escape from its confines onto the open country of Linton Moor. Occasional waymarks send the route doubling back to the right, downstream away from the beck, and fairly effortlessly gently down across the moor to a gate at some sheep-pens. The head of Moor Lane is entered here (behind the artificial rear of the quarry), and this good surfaced track drops down between walls to meet, yet again, the B6265. Cross straight over and up a steep little pull of the lane's continuation, a super leafy way that surmounts the gentle brow to meet a firmer track. This takes over to lead down the other side, bridging the now grassy former railway and emerging onto Lauradale Lane. Linton is just a minute or so ahead.

ALONG THE WAY

• **Linton** is generally accepted as being one of Northern England's most attractive villages, and not without good reason. A rich assortment of limestone buildings stand in very laid-back fashion, none wishing to crowd the spacious green. Nearest is the whitewashed little hostelry, whose name recalls a local benefactor. Richard Fountaine made his money in London, but in his will he remembered Linton by paying for the 'hospital' at the end of the green. This 18th century building remains in use as almshouses. Through the green runs lovely Linton Beck, crossed in quick succession by a road bridge, a ford, a clapper bridge and most strikingly, a fine arched packhorse bridge.

• **Thorpe** is a farming hamlet with an elusiveness that is legendary, for it quite likely kept its people and their livestock hidden from the marauding Scots. Romantically but appropriately titled 'Thorpe in the Hollow', it shelters between reef knolls and below the overpowering Thorpe Fell, part of Barden Moor. A wooded enclosure forms the village 'centre'.

• **Cracoe** is a little settlement marking the barely discernible watershed between Wharfedale and Airedale. The long, low white-walled Devonshire Arms has a good few years' history behind it, and like several others in the vicinity it bears the arms of the family whose moor rises behind. Cracoe Fell is crowned by the great landmark of its war memorial.

• **Rylstone** is a tiny village with much of interest. Alongside the main road is the attractive pond, fringed in April by daffodils, and once the village green. Near St. Peter's church was the home of the Norton family, who took part in 1536 in the Pilgrimage of Grace, and three years later the Rising of the North. There is an old milestone rarely seen now, plum on the junction across from the pond. Crowning the fell high above is the prominent landmark of Rylstone Cross, erected to celebrate the Paris treaty of 1813.

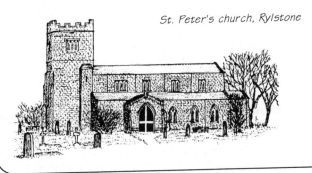

St. Peter's church, Rylstone

⑤ BORDLEY & MASTILES LANE

START Threshfield   grid ref. SD 989636
Start from the village green opposite the pub. Limited parking on the adjacent side roads or on the Burnsall or Grassington roads.

DISTANCE 12 miles/19km
Off road 8 miles/12½km   **On road** 4 miles/6½km

TERRAIN A memorable circuit with heather moorland leading to dry limestone uplands. The uphill work is split into several gentle sections, with just one moist stretch on Threshfield Moor itself.

ORDNANCE SURVEY MAPS
1:50,000 - Landranger 98, Wensleydale & Upper Wharfedale
1:25,000 - Explorer OL2, Yorkshire Dales South/West

REFRESHMENTS
Pub at start.

S Leave **Threshfield** by heading south along the main road, over Threshfield Bridge and up the hill behind to quickly escape by a narrow unsigned road on the right. Moor Lane rises steadily to lose its surface at a junction: from here look back over Threshfield to Buckden Pike and Great Whernside further up the dale, and across to Grass Wood, Grassington, Simon's Seat and Cracoe Fell. Continue along the rough lane to a gate onto **Threshfield Moor**.

Of several departing tracks take the main one to the right, which runs as a delightful green way before climbing steadily and more roughly through the heather. Keep left as directed at a fork, and the track curves up to contour around the moor. As a string of stone shooting butts take shape on the left, the track is vacated as it swings up to run on the right: our less firm way keeps left, passing between the butts to run on, somewhat softly and moistly, to an obvious wall junction ahead.

Pass through the gate and the track swings around to the left, soon descending the less moist and gentler Boss Moor. A slight rise on a now firmer surface merges with a track from the left to meet an unfenced road (Boss Moor Lane) at old small quarries overlooking the Winterburn Valley. Winterburn Reservoir is prominent below, backed

24

by the more distant Pendle Hill. Here double back right on the road, which after a cattle-grid winds steeply down to run on to end at a fork and bridge at **Lainger House**. The resuming track past the farm quickly becomes unenclosed to ascend through the fields, levelling out to run on past a small plantation with Bordley Hall Farm in the valley below. At the valley head are the limestone heights of Malham Moor. After a second plantation **Bordley** is finally fully revealed sheltering in its hollow just ahead. Typically the track has to drop down to a tiny stream to re-ascend the wallside opposite to enter the hamlet as a stony farmyard track.

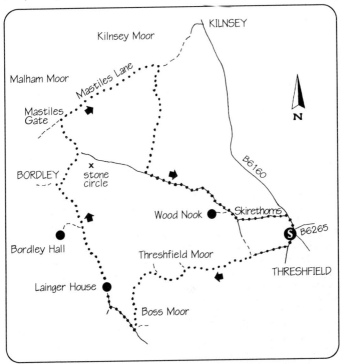

In the hamlet turn right to follow the unsurfaced access road away, immediately climbing unkindly steeply to a brow to look back over the hamlet. A short drop is then made to a gate at a crossroads of bridleways. If you've had enough, then turn right on the continuing access road: at the gate just ahead it becomes surfaced, makes a short climb, then initially as Malham Moor Lane enjoys a long, largely traffic-free downhill return to Threshfield.

However, that pleasure also awaits those who take in the full run, which now goes on to Mastiles Lane and some fine open country. So from the crossroads go straight ahead on a faint grassy, level wallside track running along to meet **Mastiles Lane** at Mastiles Gate. Pass through and follow the now enclosed lane, firmly surfaced for a very short rise to its (and the ride's) summit at 1388ft/423m. This is a cracking moment, and the descent towards Wharfedale begins at once, a good mile or so of rapid descent that should be taken steadily to savour the setting. At the bottom the track passes through a gate (and sometimes a stream) in a dip, and as it becomes unenclosed, double back sharply right on a very green enclosed way. This quickly emerges into an extensive limestone pasture, and even more quickly begins ascending it as a sometimes quite faint broad green way.

Though it appears daunting this is quite a steady gradient on a good surface, and can be punctuated with the excuse of the good retrospective views back towards Great Whernside. Towards the top it levels out to run on to a gate, then one final steady pull leads to a marker post on a brow. The climbing is over! The track then makes a welcome descent across the pasture to a gate onto Malham Moor Lane. Simply turn left to finish: before the lane gets to grips with the real descent, note on the right the twin dark entrances of Calf Hole

(also known as Height Cave), which has yielded evidence of occupation by Bronze Age and Iron Age man. Be prepared for one or two steeper sections as the road drops down into **Skirethorns** before emerging as Skirethorns Lane (absorbing the quarry access road) to join the valley road just north of the village.

Village stocks and Old Hall, Threshfield

26

ALONG THE WAY

- **Threshfield** is a disjointed village scattered around the junction of the Skipton-Grassington road with the main updale road. The 'new' part of the village - with its striking Roman Catholic church of modern design - is along the Grassington road, but it is the more interesting old corner we visit. Solid stone cottages and farm buildings overlook a quaint, triangular green, enclosed by walls and shrouded in trees. Inside are some stocks and the flowers of spring. Alongside the green note the stone lintel of the old Post office, dated 1651. Just across the main road is the popular Old Hall inn, whose title serves to indicate its original purpose.
- **Threshfield Moor** displays much evidence of a former colliery, where poor quality coal was won to fuel the lead smelting operations just across the valley on Grassington Moor. The first section on the moor passes between numerous grassed over spoilheaps, now looking somewhat incongruous. The heathery upper section of the moor supports grouse shooting.
- **Lainger House** sports a fine old gable and a 1673 datestone, and marks the termination of the public road penetrating the Winterburn Valley. A traditional red telephone box here has probably only survived due to its isolation! Note also the tiny grassy stone arched bridge just upstream. The stone carved 'Bordley' sign refers only to the fact that we have entered Bordley parish: Bordley itself is still a good mile and a half distant.
- **Bordley** is a lonely outpost where sheep farming continues from its days as a monastic township. Despite being over a thousand feet above sea level, the ancient hamlet cleverly shelters in a fold of the hills. The solid stone buildings are spread around a green that is workmanlike rather than picturesque. A quick glance at the map reveals the remarkable number of pathways converging here, a fair indication of Bordley's past importance. Though 'road' access is from Wharfedale, Bordley is actually part of Airedale, as the Winterburn Valley's beck joins the Aire on the edge of Gargrave.

Bordley Stone Circle

Bordley can also lay claim to its own stone circle, though don't come expecting another Stonehenge! This rather modest example consists of three tightly-huddled stones, all that remains of a larger circle thought to date from the Bronze Age. It is located just over a wall from the first stretch of surfaced road climbing away from the bridle-crossroads after leaving the hamlet.

> • **Mastiles Lane** is the 'big name' in green roads of the Dales. Riding the rolling limestone uplands, it gave access to the valuable sheep grazing grounds of Malham for the Fountains' monks, indeed continuing ultimately to their lands in Borrowdale, in Cumberland. Packmen and drovers would have taken advantage of it, though the confining walls that seem integral to its atmosphere would not have been known to its monastic patrons. During our descent the impressive view over Wharfedale is dominated by Great Whernside; Conistone village is straight across beneath a fine limestone landscape (including most of the course of Route 6); other notable features are Bastow Wood, Simon's Seat and Grassington.
>
> *Mastiles Lane*
>
>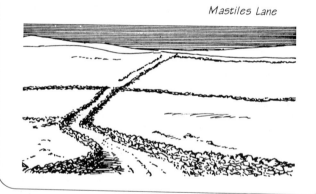

Skirethorns is a tiny hamlet on the edge of Threshfield, with a beautiful corner where attractive cottages are fronted by a well maintained green. Just behind, but out of sight from here, is the massive limestone quarry. Before joining the main road, note to the right the course of a little mineral line that ran from the quarry to the abandoned railhead at Threshfield (though known as Grassington station).

START Conistone   grid ref. SD 980674
Start from the village centre. Parking is fairly limited, but there is usually ample room on the wide section of road between the village and Conistone Bridge.

DISTANCE 8 miles/12¾km
Off road 7½ miles/12km   **On road** ½ mile/¾km

TERRAIN Good surfaces throughout. After the steep initial ascent, the entire route is on a good grassy way which becomes a firm upland track. A rare there-and-back route, and while there's no alternative, neither is one necessary as this is a joy to return on.

ORDNANCE SURVEY MAPS
1:50,000 - Landranger 98, Wensleydale & Upper Wharfedale
1:25,000 - Explorer OL2, Yorkshire Dales South/West

REFRESHMENTS
None! Pub and cafe at Kilnsey across the river.

S From the road junction beneath the maypole in the centre of **Conistone**, follow the unsigned back road towards Kettlewell north out of the village. Just beyond the church, turn off to the right along the roughly surfaced Scot Gate Lane. Don't be deterred if the official post only states 'footpath to Middlesmoor', it is in fact a bridleway as far as we need it. After a short stony section it becomes surfaced to commence a steep pull up Wassa Hill, winding up to a gate. Here it downgrades to a standard track, still ascending through more open pasture. Sections of **Conistone Dib** are seen down to the right. This main climb eases out at a TV mast, though one steep little pull awaits before running along to a crossroads with the Dales Way path. Just off route to the right is the very head of Conistone Dib.

Resuming, the now greener track gently rises between limestone scars. That on the left supports a particularly notable limestone pavement, across which stands an old limekiln. Also passed just beyond is a circular dewpond, created to provide liquid refreshment for cattle on these dry limestone pastures. Now as the Bycliffe Road the way becomes enclosed again to climb to a junction. Remain on

29

the main track by turning sharp right, again ignoring the signpost's 'footpath' claim. A gentle run to Kelber Gate precedes the last climb, a steep haul up to another gate. Entering rougher pasture a final little slope leads onto the high point of 1404ft/428m. Ahead is wide sweeping country: a super ride leads along easy, undulating terrain to look down upon the great bowl of Bycliffe.

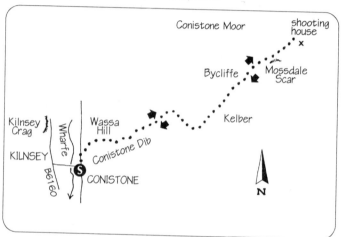

The final stage awaits as continually easy riding drops gently down across this setting of upland grandeur and on to **Mossdale**. Before long the great cliff of Mossdale Scar is alongside, very much the place to linger and savour the scene as well as some refreshment perhaps. Although one can return from here, it is but a few minutes further along the track to call a halt where the bridleway leaves to ford Mossdale Beck, with a solid shooting house on the other bank. There is little point advancing any further. The bridleway, for the record, resumes across impractical moorland terrain to climb to the watershed at Sandy Gate, which is also the National Park boundary. Here the bridleway literally ends, as the route is classed as footpath only for the long descent to Nidderdale.

Return to Conistone by the outward route, almost entirely downhill and with outstanding views across Wharfedale. Particularly notable as height is lost is the line of Mastiles Lane (see Route 5) marching up the opposite slopes above the dark overhang of Kilnsey Crag.

ALONG THE WAY

• **Conistone** is an attractive little village avoided by the main road, just half a mile distant across the River Wharfe at Kilnsey: even from this distance the famous crag loses none of its grandeur. Every piece of stone in Conistone's cottages matches the natural landscape of the village's hinterland. Though restored a century ago, the hidden church of St. Mary retains some Norman features.

St. Mary's church, Conistone

• **Conistone Dib** is a classic example of a dry limestone valley, narrowing to very distinctive rock-girt termini. A superb limestone pavement sits just above.

• **Mossdale** is an almost hidden upland valley, drained by the sizeable Mossdale Beck which plunges underground in the shadow of the substantial Mossdale Scar. This is Mossdale Cavern, scene of a 1967 tragedy when six potholers perished in heavy floodwater: a memorial stone in the churchyard makes a fitting last stop as you re-enter the village. Menacing enough is the scar itself, for a mighty chunk of it collapsed as recently as 1999.

Mossdale Scar

LOG OF THE RIDES

No	Date	Start	Finish	Notes
1				
2				
3				
4				
5				
6				